Contents

Numbers 1 - 5

1

uno

2

due

3

tre

4

quattro

5

cinque

Read the Italian numbers as you colour the pictures.

How many strawberries are there?
(Write the number in Italian.)

a)

b)

 tre

_____

_____

c)

d)

_____

_____

e) _____

1	2	3	4	5
uno	due	tre	quattro	cinque

2

Draw the correct number of sweets

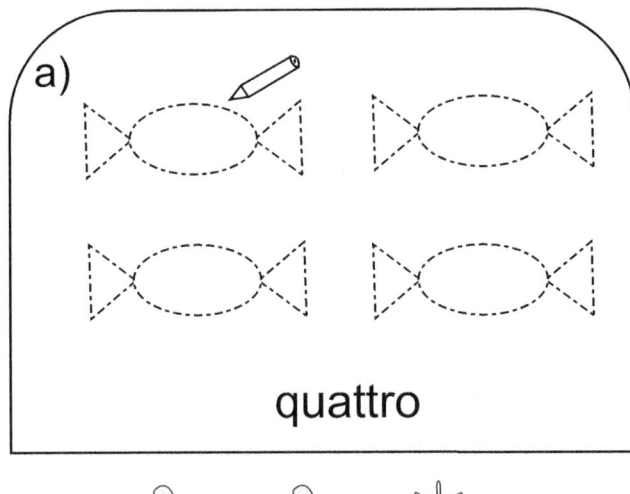

a)

quattro

b)

due

c)

cinque

d)

tre

e)

uno

 | **1** | **2** | **3** | **4** | **5** |

uno   due   tre   quattro   cinque

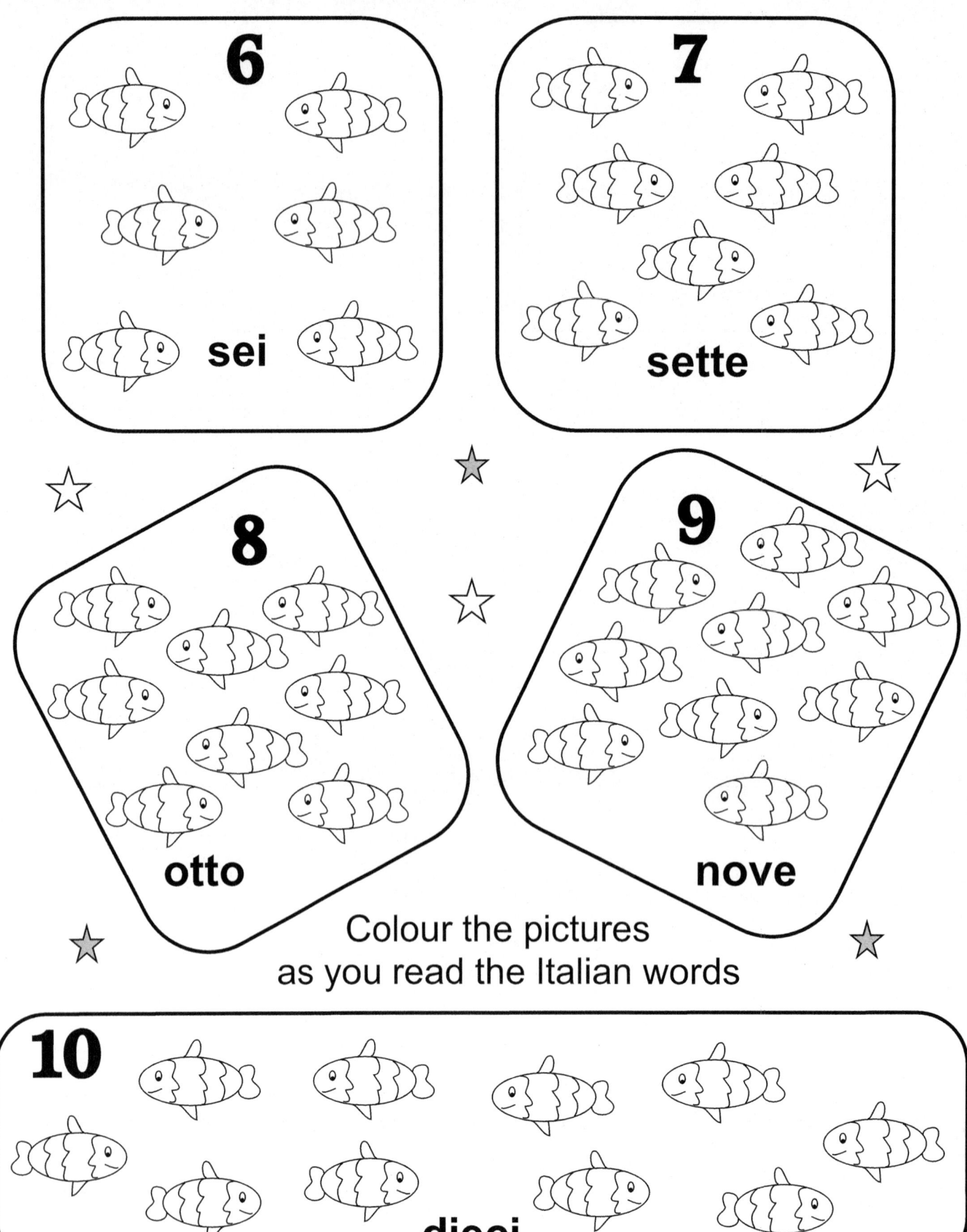

6 sei

7 sette

8 otto

9 nove

Colour the pictures
as you read the Italian words

10 dieci

How many are there?

Write the number in Italian:

a)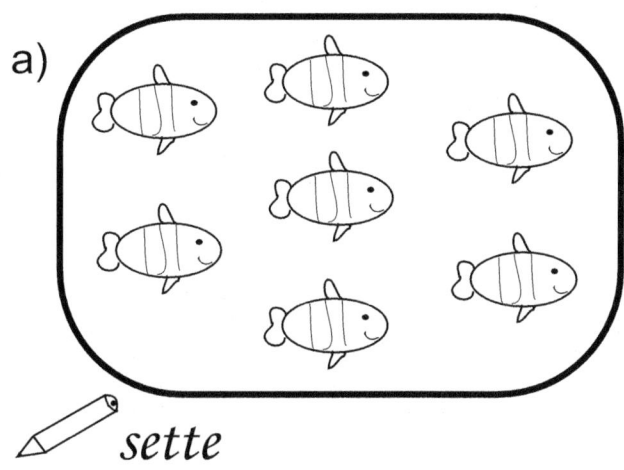

✏️ *sette*

_____

b)

_____

c)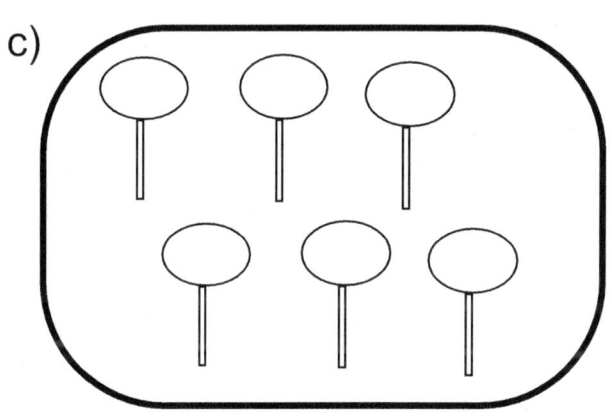

_____

d)

_____

e)

_____

6	7	8	9	10
sei	sette	otto	nove	dieci

Draw the correct number of balloons

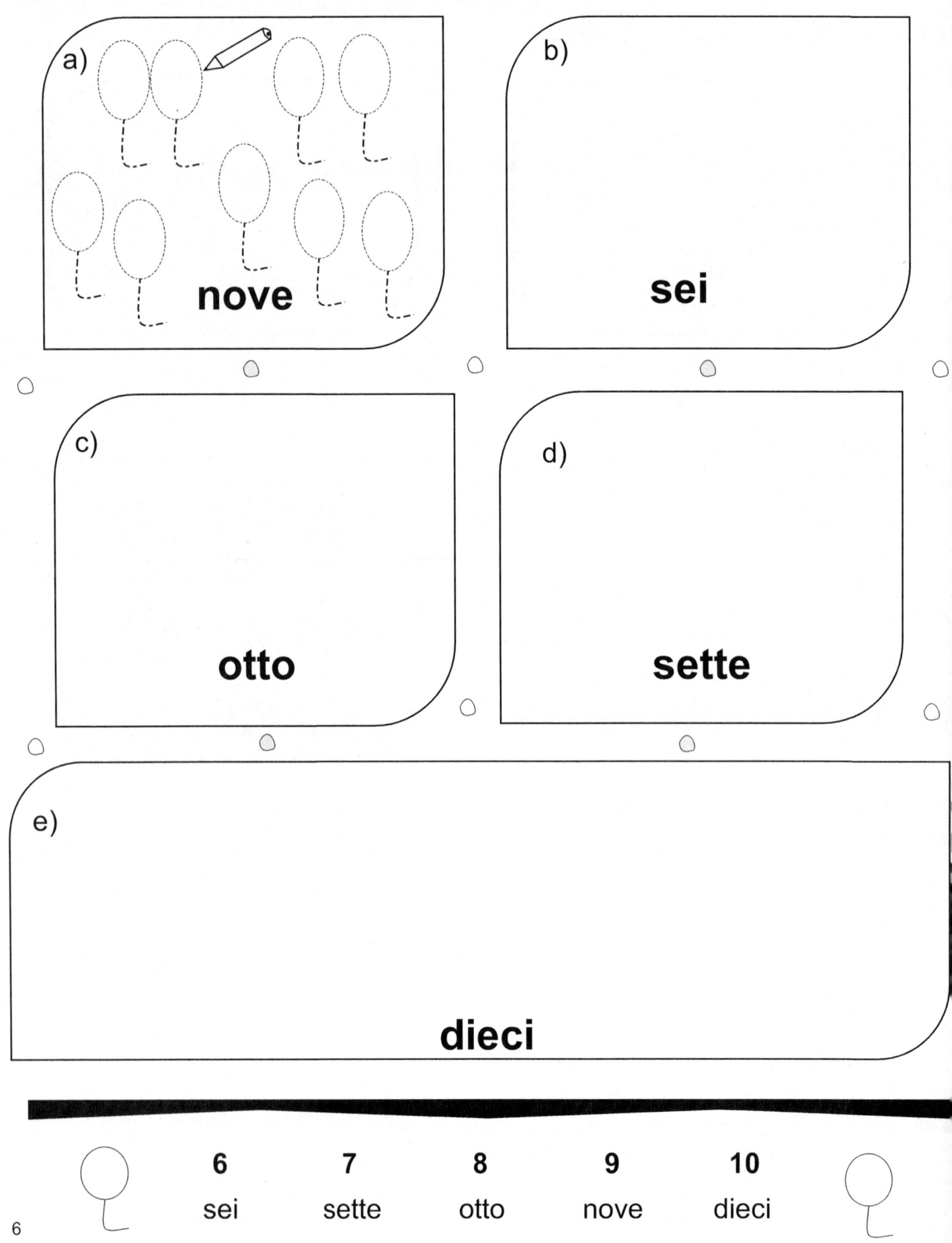

a) nove

b) sei

c) otto

d) sette

e) dieci

6	7	8	9	10
sei	sette	otto	nove	dieci

Colour in the odd numbers

The odd numbers are: uno, tre, cinque, sette, nove

The toy shop

il robot

il pallone

la bambola

la macchina

il trenino

Colour the pictures as you read the Italian words.

il robot   il pallone   la bambola   la macchina   il trenino

Look at the pictures below, and draw a line to the correct Italian word:

il robot

il pallone

il trenino

la bambola

la macchina

Which toy is it?

Draw the pictures and copy the Italian words:

1) la bambola

_____

2) il robot

_____

3) il pallone

_____

4) il trenino

_____

  il robot   il pallone  la bambola il trenino

At the toy shop

Follow the lines from each child to discover what the children want to buy at the toy shop. Write the Italian word for the toy on the line by each child:

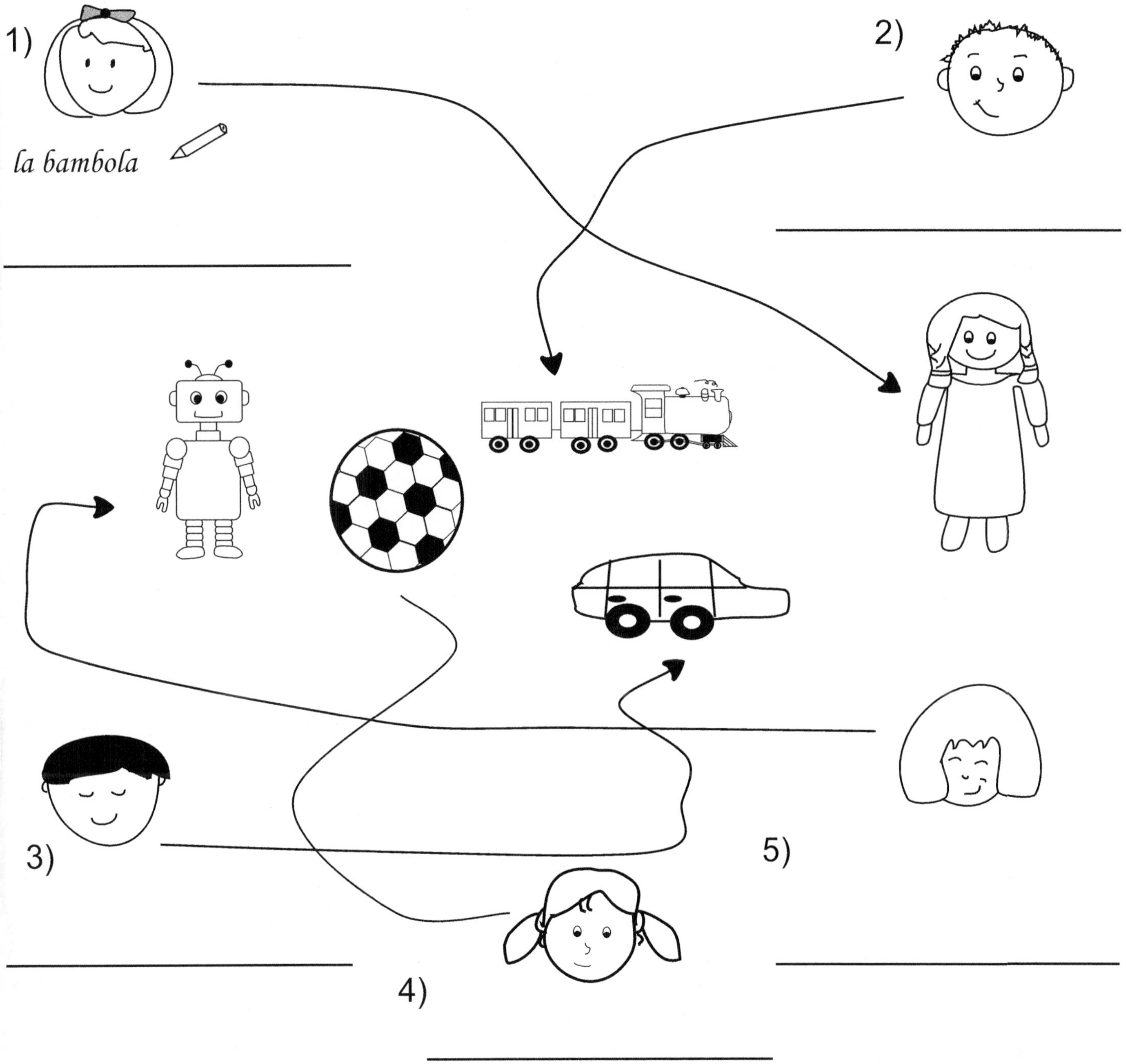

1) *la bambola*

2) _____

_____

3) _____

4) _____

5) _____

 il robot    il pallone    la bambola    la macchina    il trenino

Greetings

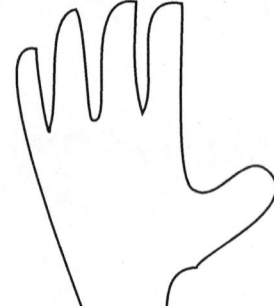

Ciao

(Hi / Bye)

Buon giorno

(Good day)

Buona sera

(Good evening)

Buona notte

(Good night)

Introducing yourself!

Mi chiamo Marco.

Mi chiamo Anna.

Introduce yourself by writing **Mi chiamo** and then write your name. (Mi chiamo = My name is)

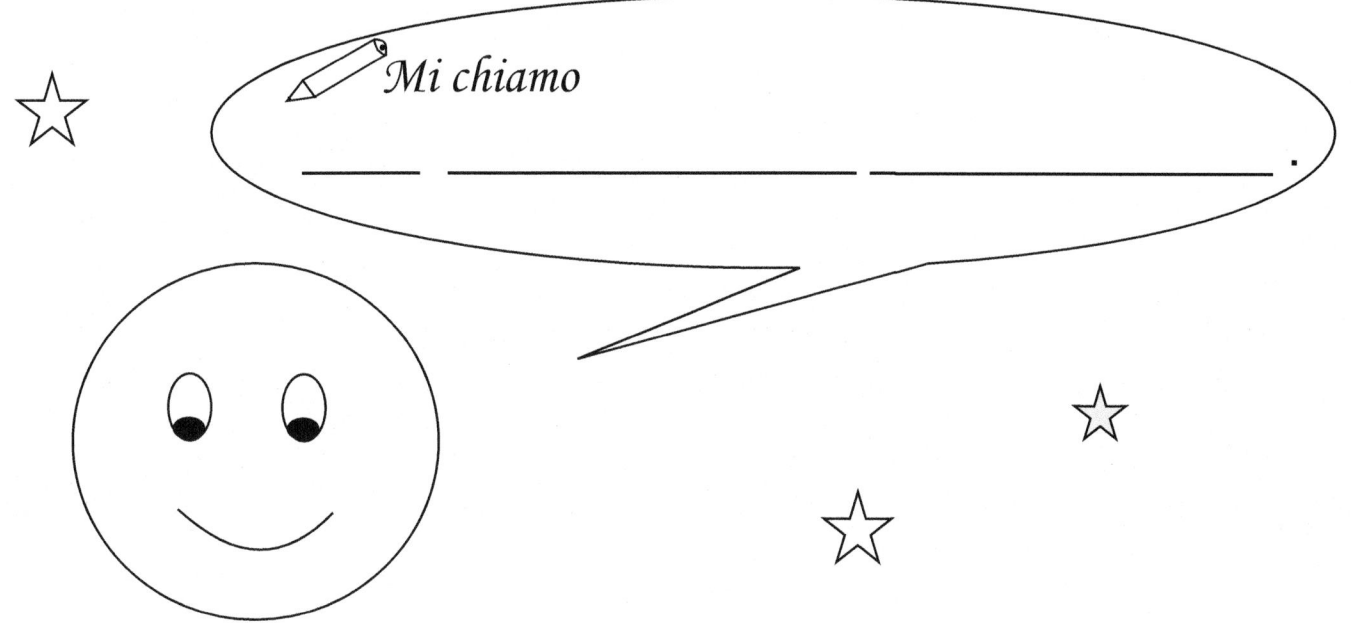

Mi chiamo

____ _____ _____.

Useful words

per favore - please

no - no

sì - yes

grazie - thank you

How do you say the following in Italian?

 *per   favore*

1) please   _____   _____

2) yes   _____

3) thank you   _____

4) no   _____

Saying goodbye

> Ciao.
>
> Arrivederci.

To say goodbye you could either say **ciao,** or **arrivederci** if you will see the person again.

The children below are saying goodbye in Italian.
Write either **ciao** or **arrivederci** in the speech bubbles:

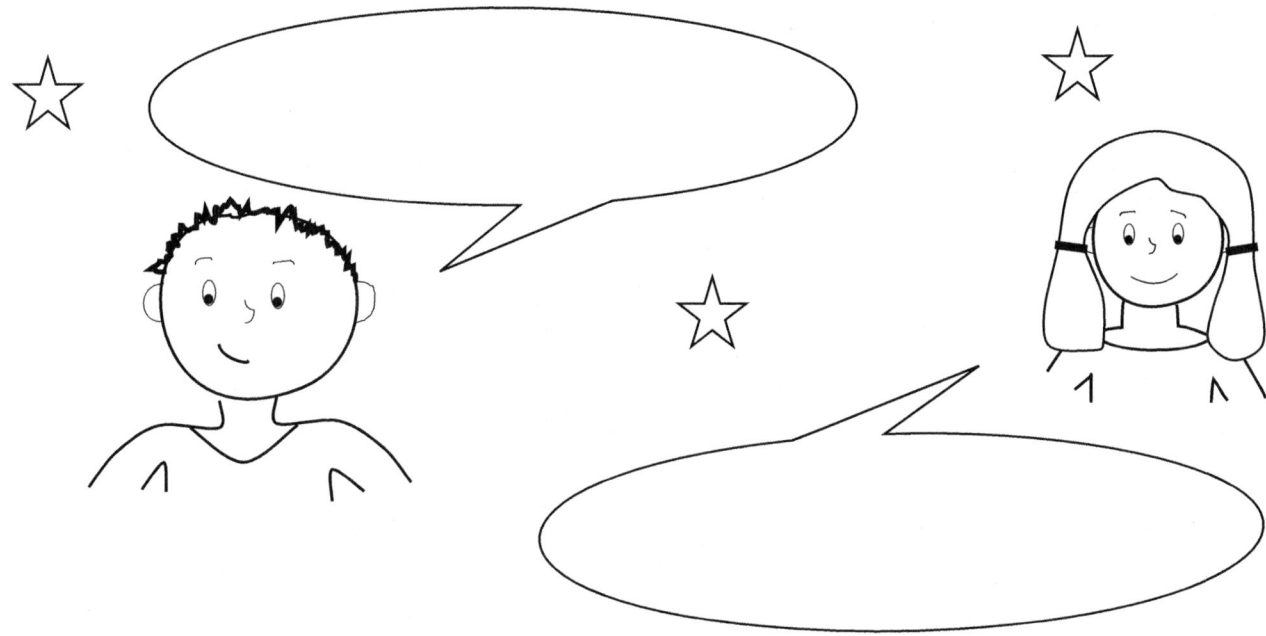

What is it in Italian?

Draw a line from the English word to the correct Italian word:

Hi

yes

please

my name is

thank you

Goodbye

sì

grazie

Ciao

per favore

Arrivederci

mi chiamo

Word search

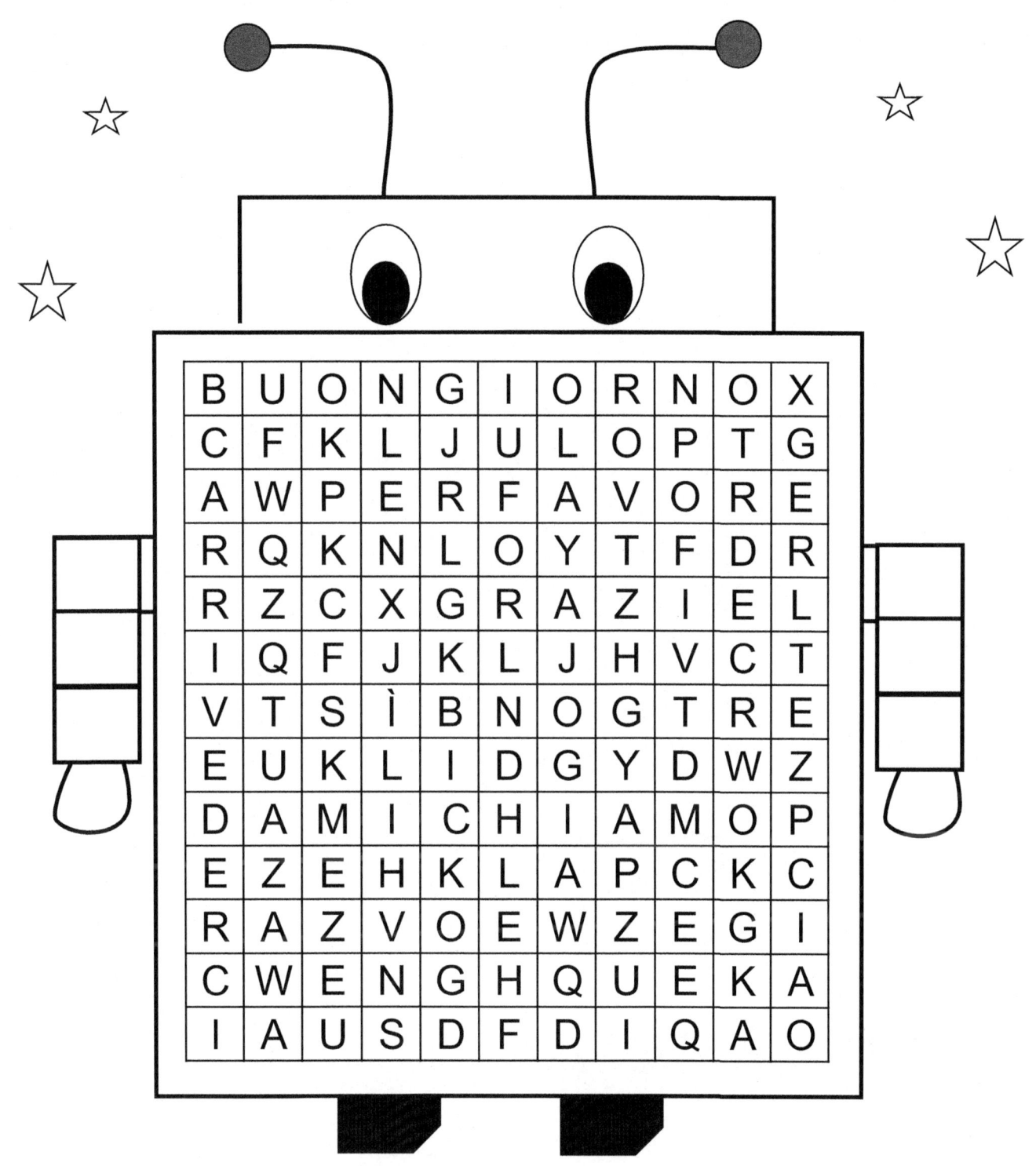

B	U	O	N	G	I	O	R	N	O	X
C	F	K	L	J	U	L	O	P	T	G
A	W	P	E	R	F	A	V	O	R	E
R	Q	K	N	L	O	Y	T	F	D	R
R	Z	C	X	G	R	A	Z	I	E	L
I	Q	F	J	K	L	J	H	V	C	T
V	T	S	Ì	B	N	O	G	T	R	E
E	U	K	L	I	D	G	Y	D	W	Z
D	A	M	I	C	H	I	A	M	O	P
E	Z	E	H	K	L	A	P	C	K	C
R	A	Z	V	O	E	W	Z	E	G	I
C	W	E	N	G	H	Q	U	E	K	A
I	A	U	S	D	F	D	I	Q	A	O

Find these words:

CIAO   BUON GIORNO   SÌ   PER FAVORE

GRAZIE   MI CHIAMO   NO   ARRIVEDERCI

UNO   DUE   TRE

17

A trip to the beach!

Read the Italian words as you colour the pictures:

il sole

la spiaggia
(the beach)

un castello

un gelato

il mare

What is it?

Read the Italian words and draw a picture:

1)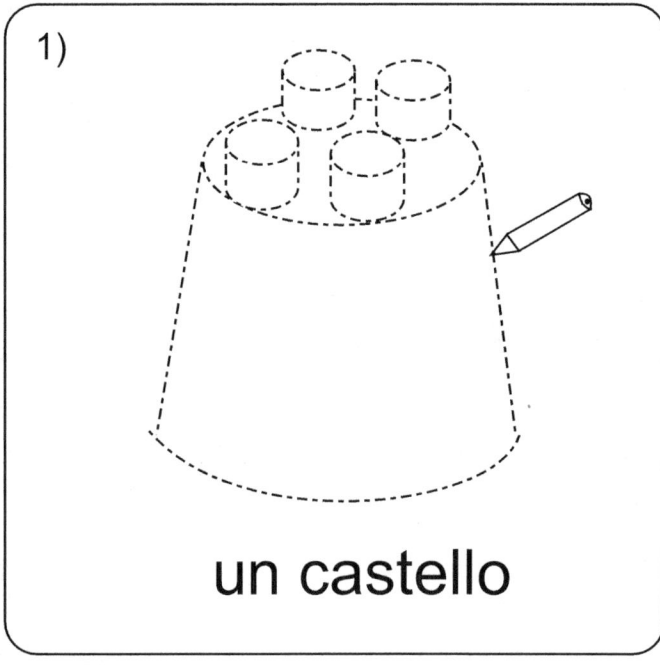

un castello

2)

il sole

3)

un gelato

4)

il mare

il sole

il mare

un gelato

un castello

Copy the Italian words:

il sole

il sole 🖉

_____

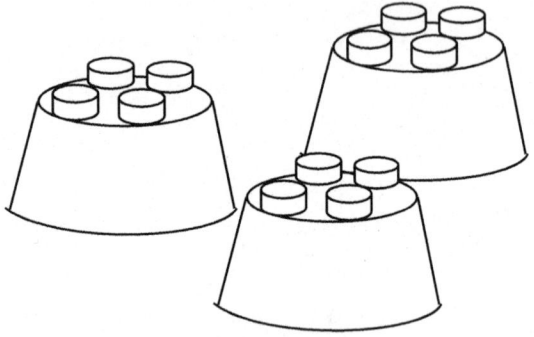

un castello

_____

un gelato

_____

il mare

_____

la spiaggia

_____

Which word is it?

Draw a line between the pictures and the Italian words:

la spiaggia

il sole

il mare

un gelato

un castello

il sole   il mare   la spiaggia   un gelato   un castello

Colour the animals as you read the Italian words

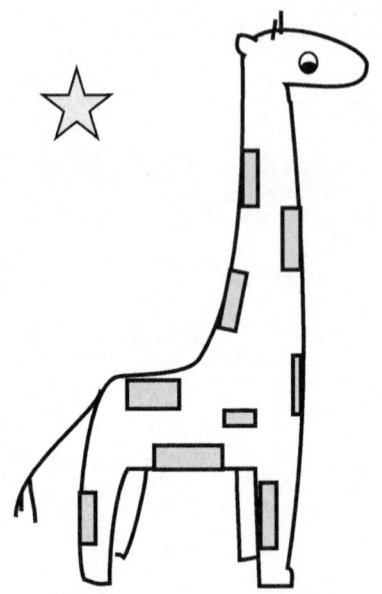

la giraffa

l'elefante

il leone

la tigre

il serpente

22

What animal is it?

Write the Italian words for the animals:

1)   2)

la giraffa

_____ _____   _____ _____

 3)

_____ _____

4)  5)

_____ _____   _____ _____

la giraffa   la tigre   l'elefante   il leone   il serpente

Circle the correct word

1) la giraffa   la tigre   l'elefante

2) la tigre   l'elefante   il leone

3) la tigre   la giraffa   il serpente

4) il leone   la tigre   l'elefante

5) l'elefante   il serpente   il leone

What is it called in Italian?

Complete the words using the following vowels:

 a e i

1)

il **l _ o n _**

2)

la **t _ g r _**

3)

la **g _ r _ f f _**

4)

l' **_ l _ f _ n t _**

25

The countryside

la farfalla

il sole

la foresta

la fattoria

i fiori

Copy the Italian words

il sole

il sole

_____

la fattoria

_____

la farfalla

_____

 la foresta

_____

i fiori

_____

What is it called in Italian?

Circle the correct Italian word:

1)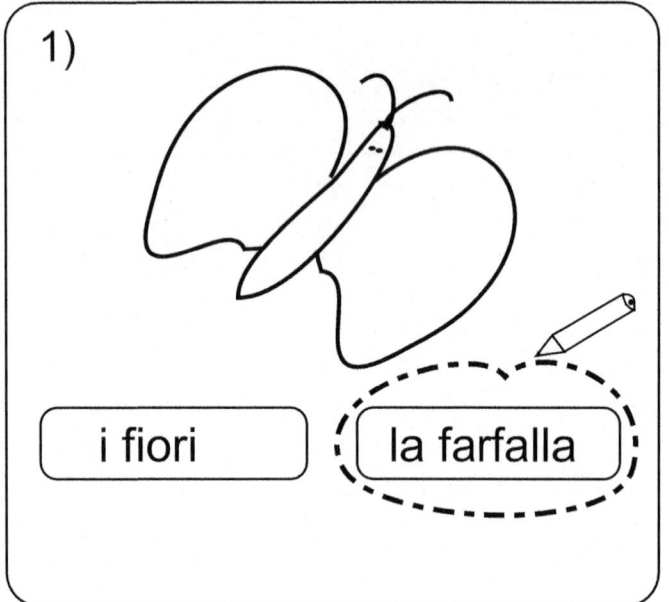

| i fiori | la farfalla |

2)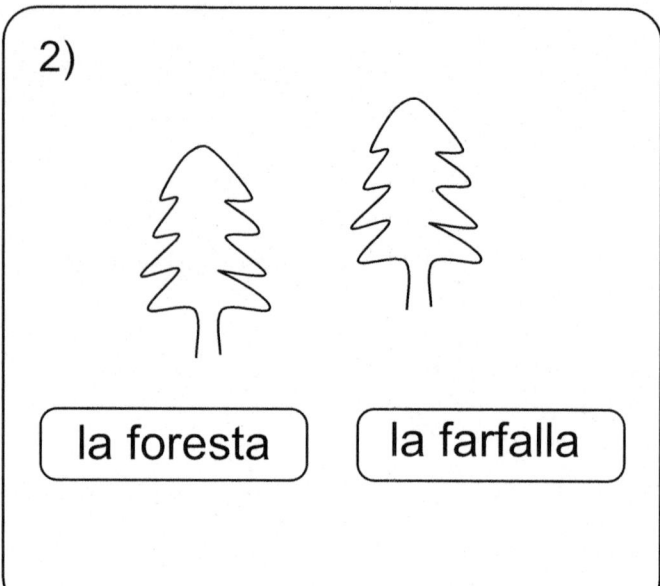

| la foresta | la farfalla |

3)

| la foresta | la fattoria |

4)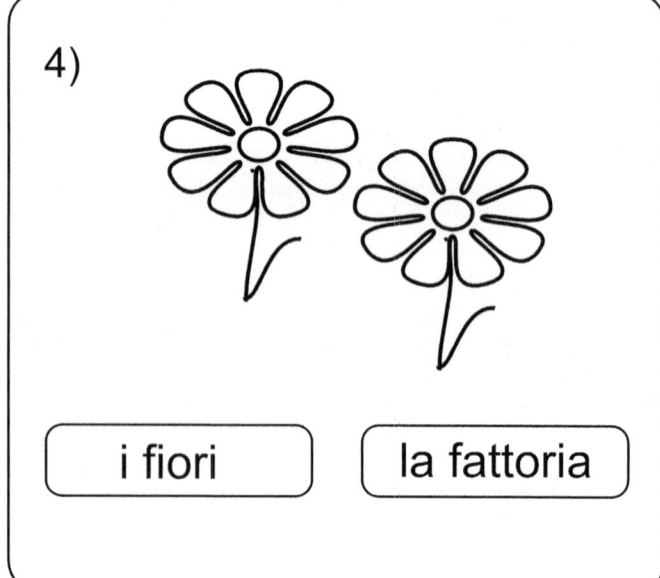

| i fiori | la fattoria |

la fattoria

i fiori

la foresta

la farfalla

Draw the following things:

1)

il sole

2)

la farfalla

3)

la foresta

4)

i fiori

5)

la fattoria

il sole   la fattoria   la farfalla   la foresta   i fiori

Colours

nero

giallo

bianco

rosso

verde

blu

Colour the picture as follows:

rosso - red   giallo - yellow   verde - green   blu - blue

(Nero (black) and bianco (white) has been done for you)

Colour the pictures using the correct colours

verde - green   rosso - red   giallo - yellow

verde

rosso

giallo

What colour is it?

Write the colour in Italian for each of the things pictured:

1)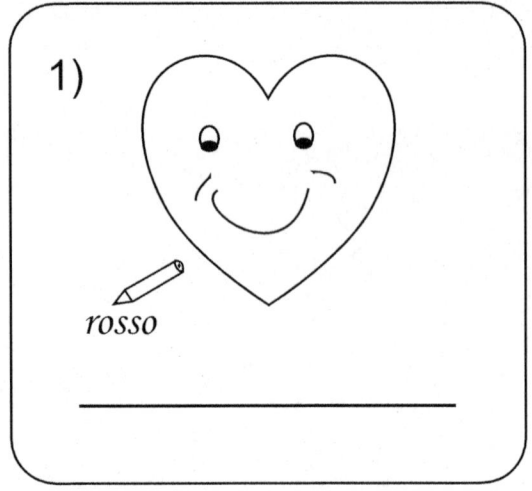
rosso

_____

_____

3)

_____

4)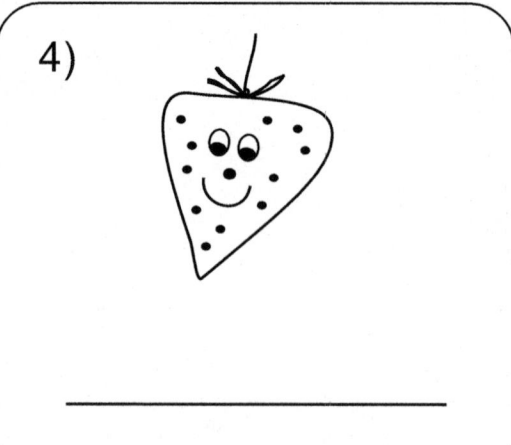

_____

5)

_____

6)

_____

verde - green   rosso - red   giallo - yellow

Colour the pictures using the correct colours:

marrone
(brown)

rosa
(pink)

blu
(blue)

What colour is it?

Write the colour of the object in Italian:

rosa - pink   marrone - brown   blu - blue

1)

rosa

_____

2)

_____

3)

_____

4)

_____

5)

_____

6)

_____

Draw a line between the colour the correct picture:

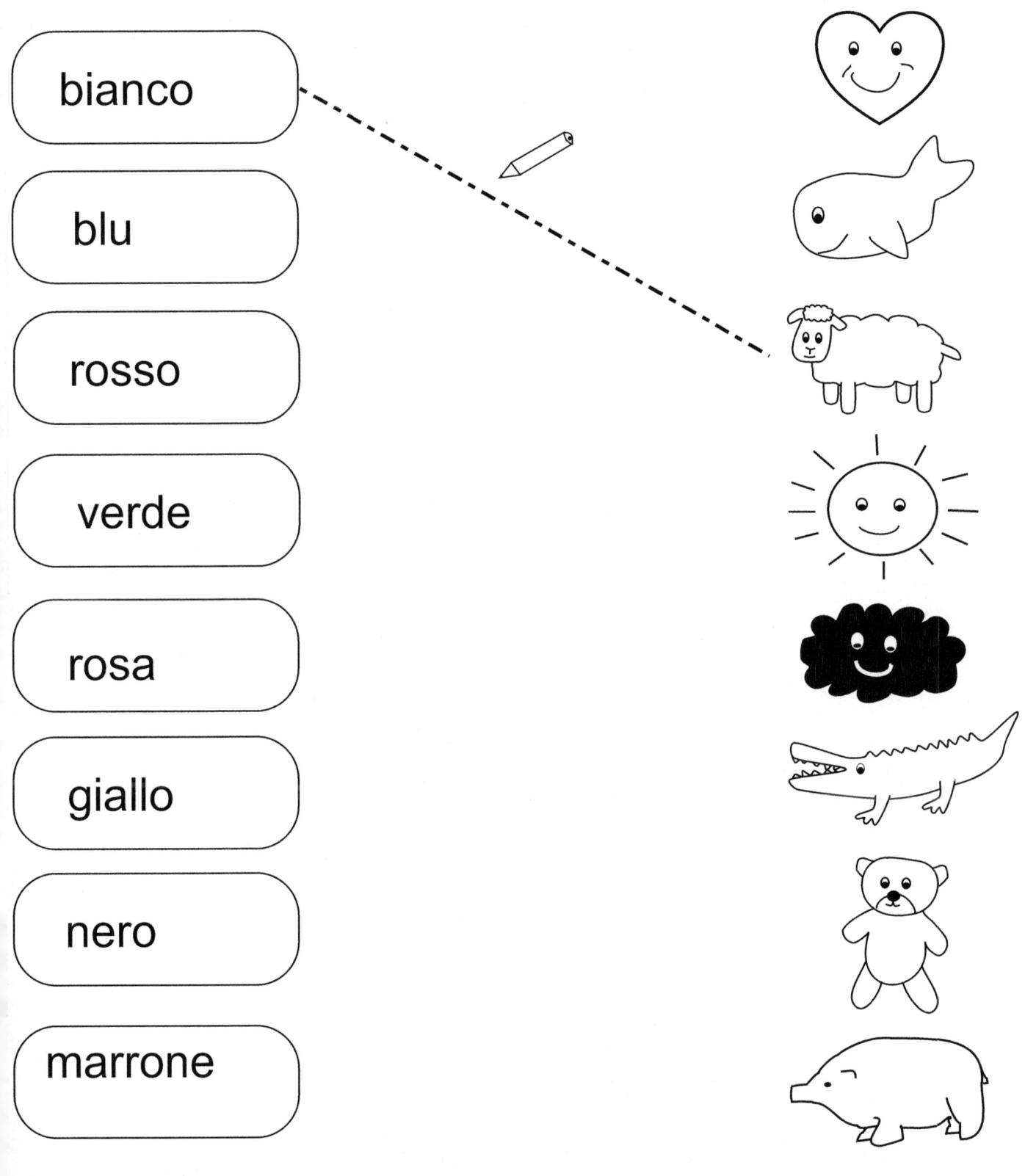

marrone - brown   blu - blue   rosso - red   bianco - white

rosa - pink   verde- green   giallo - yellow   nero - black

The Birthday party

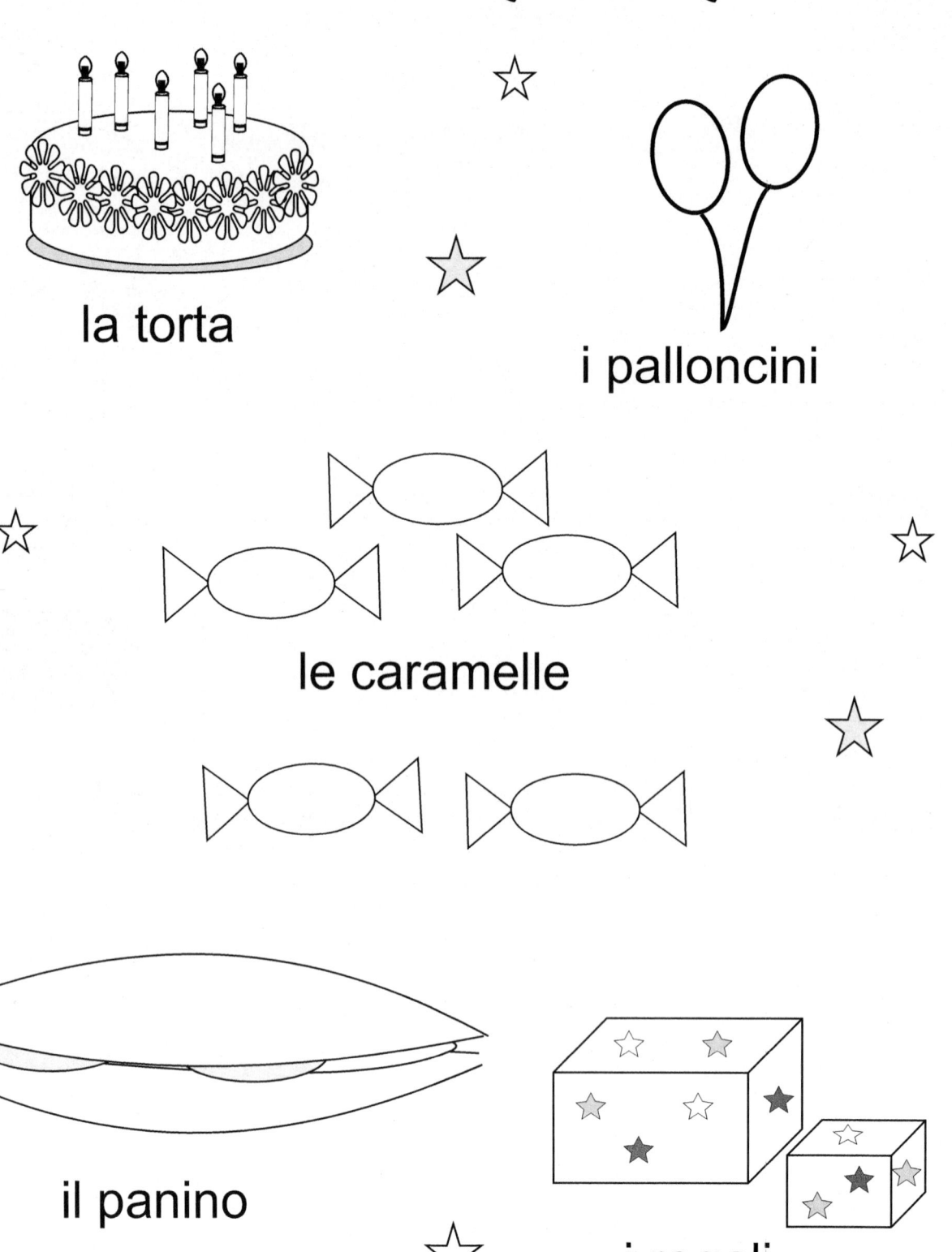

la torta

i palloncini

le caramelle

il panino

i regali

Copy the words and the pictures

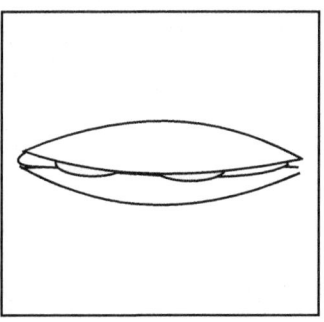

il panino

 *il panino*

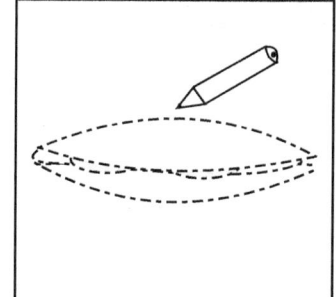

_____

la torta

_____

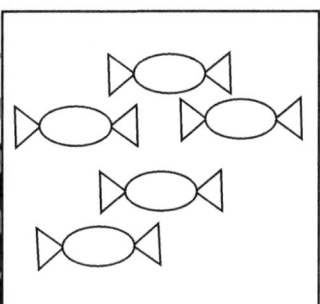

le caramelle

_____

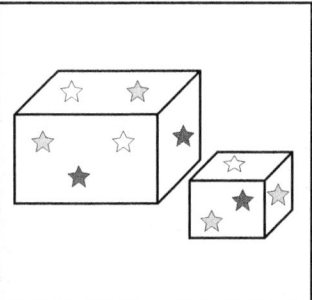

i regali

_____

i palloncini

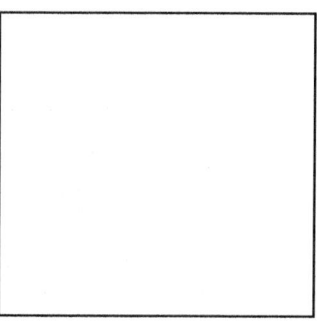

_____

What Italian word is it?

 la torta    il panino    le caramelle    i regali    i palloncini

Draw a line between the Italian word and the correct picture:

il panino

i palloncini

la torta

le caramelle

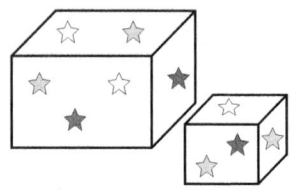

i regali

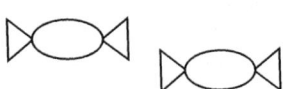

Circle the correct word

1)

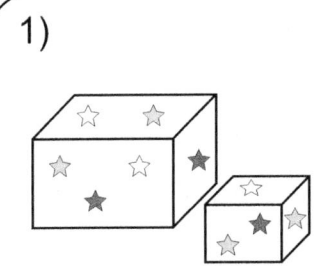 le caramelle   la torta   (i regali)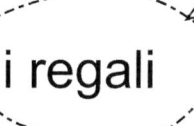

2)

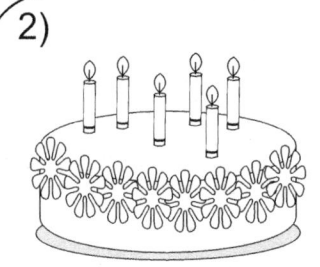 la torta   i palloncini   le caramelle

3)

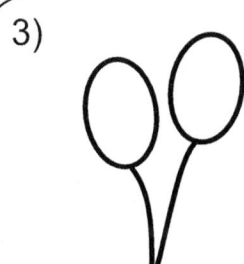 le caramelle   i palloncini   i regali

4)

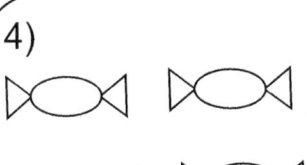 i regali   il panino   le caramelle

5)

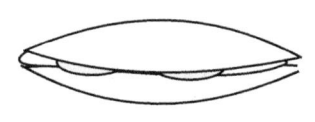 il panino   la torta   i regali

Word search

S	P	A	L	L	O	N	C	I	N	I
T	J	K	H	U	G	Y	F	B	N	M
O	I	Q	W	Z	P	A	N	I	N	O
R	E	G	M	N	L	G	F	H	Y	V
T	Q	C	A	R	A	M	E	L	L	E
A	E	R	G	L	I	D	C	U	A	J
T	J	K	U	L	G	J	Y	F	W	L
Q	X	S	A	E	G	Z	F	G	H	E
A	Z	G	Y	J	G	A	T	J	M	O
Z	E	T	H	F	R	N	F	S	R	N
R	D	W	E	I	G	R	H	P	W	E
A	G	H	G	M	T	I	G	R	E	T
E	L	E	F	A	N	T	E	P	L	Q

Find these words:

TORTA

PANINO

CARAMELLE

PALLONCINI

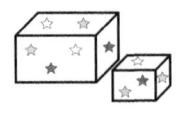

REGALI

LEONE

TIGRE

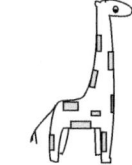

GIRAFFA

ELEFANTE

40

Italian		English	
	arrivederci		goodbye
la	bambola	the	doll
	bianco		white
	blu		blue
	buona sera		good evening
	buon giorno		good day
	buona notte		good night
le	caramelle	the	sweets
un	castello	the	castle
	ciao		hi / bye
	cinque		five
	dieci		ten
	due		two
l'	elefante	the	elephant
la	farfalla	the	butterfly
la	fattoria	the	farm
i	fiori	the	flowers
la	foresta	the	forest
un	gelato	an	ice cream
	giallo		yellow
la	giraffa	the	giraffe
	grazie		thank you
il	leone	the	lion
la	macchina	the	car
il	mare	the	sea
	marrone		brown

 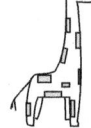 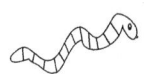 

Italian		English	
	mi chiamo		my name is
	nero		black
	no		no
	nove		nine
	otto		eight
il	palllone	the	ball
i	palloncini	the	balloons
il	panino	the	sandwich
	per favore		please
	quattro		four
i	regali	the	presents
il	robot	the	robot
	rosa		pink
	rosso		red
	sei		six
il	serpente	the	snake
	sette		seven
	sì		yes
il	sole	the	sun
la	spiaggia	the	beach
la	tigre	the	tiger
la	torta	the	cake
	tre		three
il	trenino	the	toy train
	uno		one
	verde		green

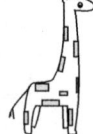
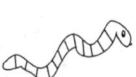

Numbers 1 - 10

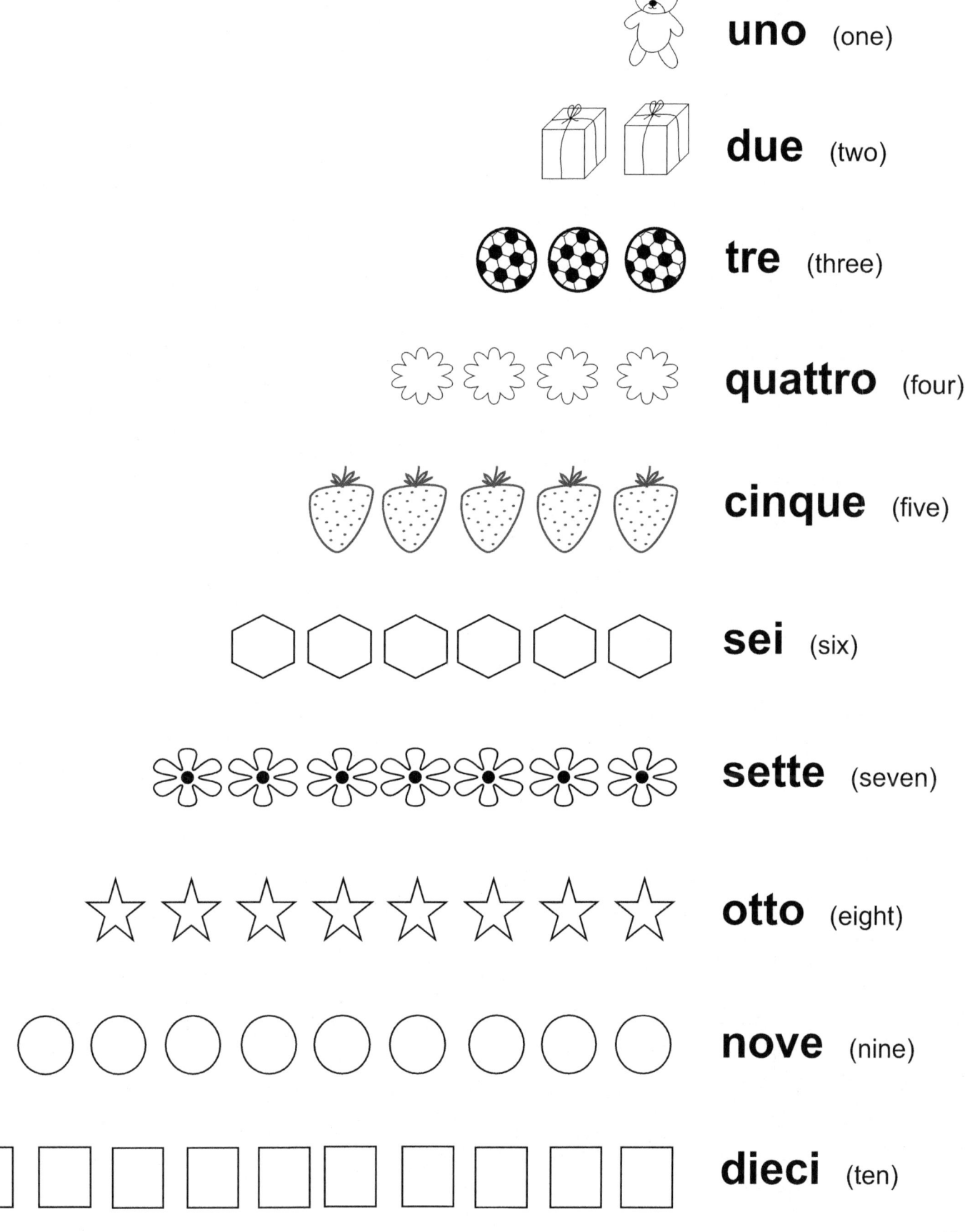

uno (one)

due (two)

tre (three)

quattro (four)

cinque (five)

sei (six)

sette (seven)

otto (eight)

nove (nine)

dieci (ten)

Comincia quì

Hai vinto!

44

Italian Word Game

For this game, you will need a dice and a counter for each player. The counters could be rubbers, cubes or you could make your own on pieces of paper.

How to play

Start at "Comincia quì", roll the dice and count that number of squares.

Say the word for the picture you land on in Italian. Take turns to roll the dice.

To win, arrive first at "Hai vinto!"

Ciao
(Hi / Bye)

1

uno
(one)

il sole
(the sun)

il panino
(the sandwich)

un gelato
(an ice cream)

l'elefante
(the elephant)

Games are a fun way to learn a foreign language! If you like games you could try the book Italian Word Games - Cool Kids Speak Italian.

Answers

Page 2

a) tre   b) due   c) quattro   d) uno   e) cinque

Page 3

The following number of sweets should be drawn:
a) four   b) two   c) five   d) three   e) one

Page 5

a) sette   b) otto   c) sei   d) nove   e) dieci

Page 6

The following number of balloons should be drawn:
a) nine   b) six   c) eight   d) seven   e) ten

Page 7

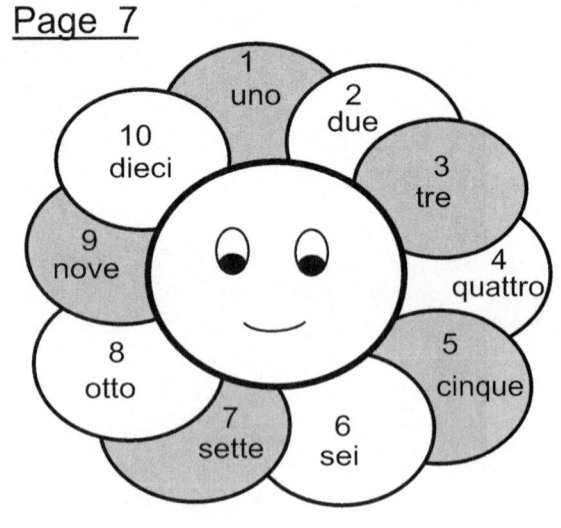

Page 9

il robot

il pallone

il trenino

la bambola

la macchina

Page 10

The following should be drawn:
1) the doll   2) the robot   3) the ball   4) the toy train

Page 11

1) la bambola   2) il trenino   3) la macchina   4) il pallone   5) il robot

Page 14

1) per favore   2) sì   3) grazie   4) no

Page 16

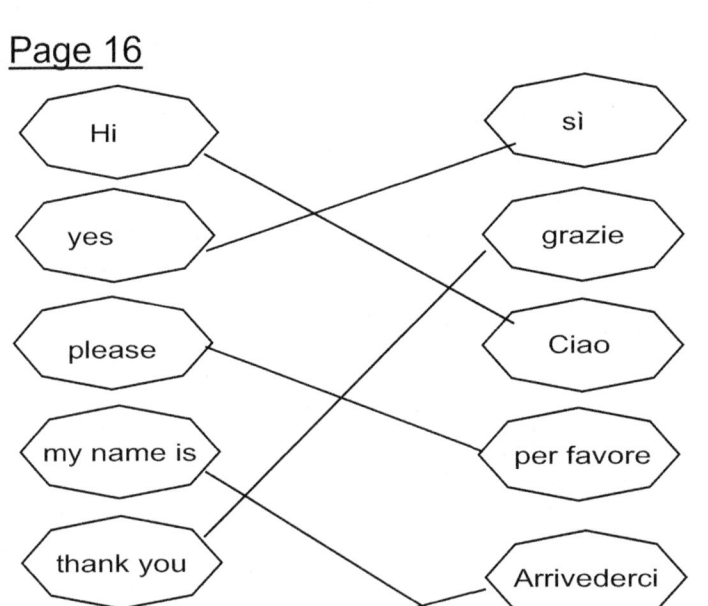

Hi — Ciao
yes — sì
please — per favore
my name is — mi chiamo
thank you — grazie
Goodbye — Arrivederci

Page 17

B	U	O	N	G	I	O	R	N	O	
A		P	E	R	F	A	V	O	R	E
R										
R			G	R	A	Z	I	E		
I										
V		S	Ì		N	O		T	R	E
E										
D		M	I	C	H	I	A	M	O	
E										C
R			O					E		I
C		N				U				A
I	U				D					O

Page 19

The following should be drawn
1) a castle   2) the sun   3) an ice cream   4) the sea

Page 21

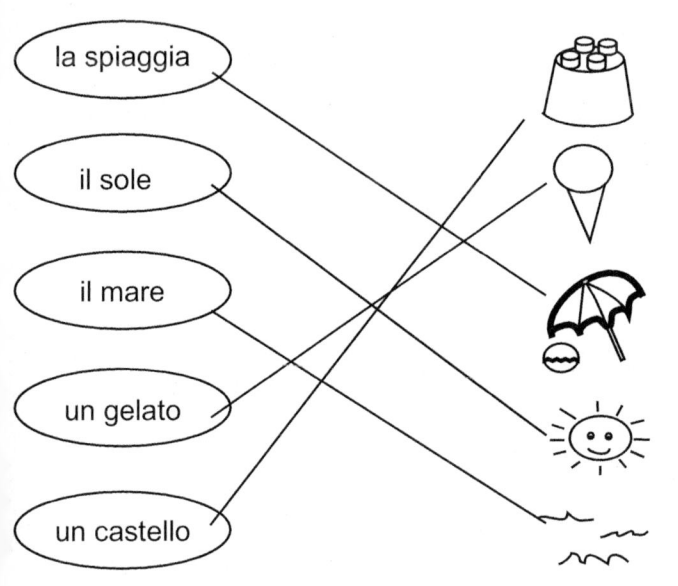

la spiaggia
il sole
il mare
un gelato
un castello

Page 23

1) la giraffa   2) la tigre   3) il serpente
4) il leone   5) l'elefante

Page 24

1) la giraffa   2) il leone   3) la tigre
4) l'elefante   5) il serpente

Page 25

1) il leone   2) la tigre   3) la giraffa
4) l'elefante

Page 28

1) la farfalla   2) la foresta   3) la fattoria
4) i fiori

Page 29

The following should be drawn:
1) the sun   2) the butterfly   3) the forest
4) the flowers   5) the farm

Page 30

The picture should be coloured as follows:
rosso = red   giallo = yellow   blu = blue   verde = green   bianco = white   nero = black

Page 31

verde = green   rosso = red   giallo = yellow

Page 32

1) rosso   2) giallo   3) verde   4) rosso
5) giallo   6) verde

Page 33

The pictures should be coloured as follows:
marrone = brown   rosa = pink   blu = blue

Page 34

1) rosa   2) marrone   3) blu   4) marrone
5) blu   6) rosa

Page 35

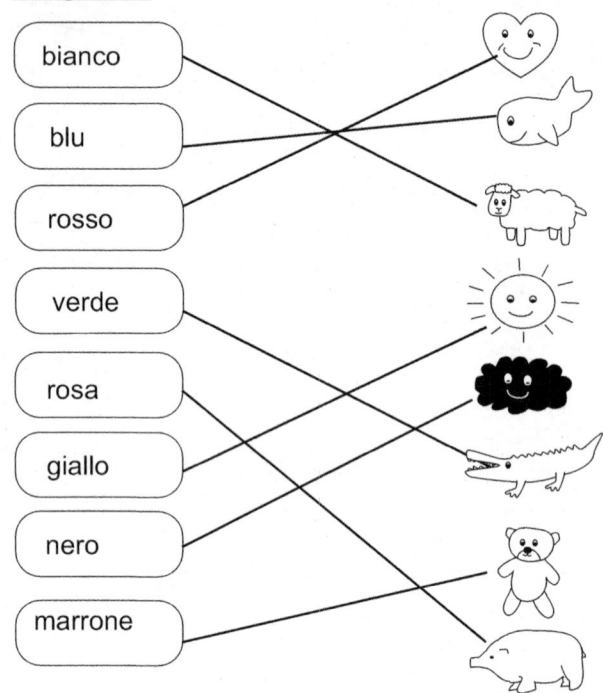

bianco
blu
rosso
verde
rosa
giallo
nero
marrone

Page 38

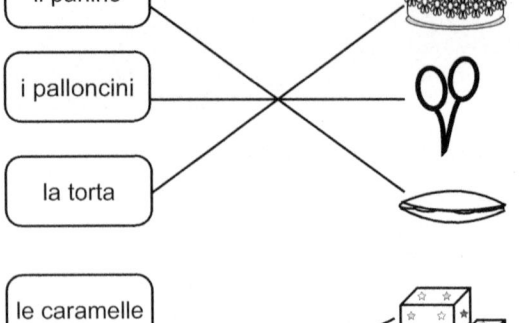
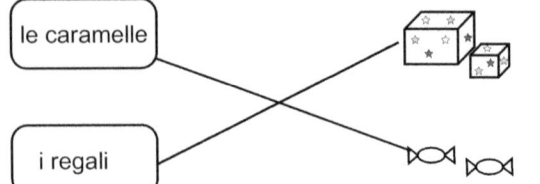

il panino
i palloncini
la torta
le caramelle
i regali

Page 39

1) i regali
2) la torta
3) i palloncini
4) le caramelle
5) il panino

Page 40

	P	A	L	L	O	N	C	I	N	I
T										
O					P	A	N	I	N	O
R										
T		C	A	R	A	M	E	L	L	E
A					I				A	
			L				F		L	
		A				F			E	
	G				A				O	
E				R					N	
R			I						E	
		G		T	I	G	R	E		
E	L	E	F	A	N	T	E			

Cool Kids Speak Italian - Book 1 by Joanne Leyland

Learning Italian is fun with the activity sheets, words searches and colouring pages in this great book. Each topic begins with a page full of images and the Italian words for the topic. The activities practise only a few of the new words at a time, and then gradually introduce simple sentence structures. At the back of the book is a snakes and ladders game, a useful Italian English word list, and the answers. ISBN: 9781914159015. Suggested age range: 7 - 11 years.

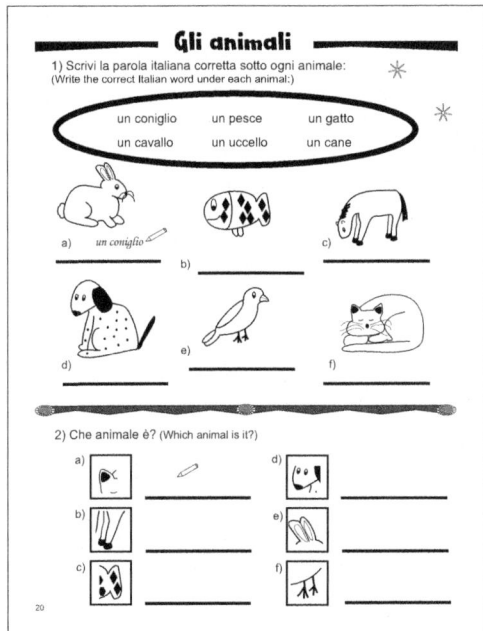

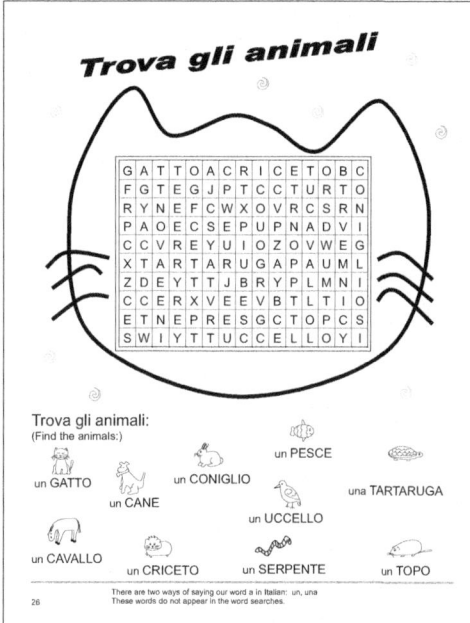

Topics include:

Greetings & Introductions

Numbers

Colours

Pet animals

Drinks

Pizzas

First 100 Words In Italian Coloring Book - Cool Kids Speak Italian by Joanne Leyland

The 100 Italian words in this brilliant book include a marvellous mix of favourite children's characters (for example a fairy, a dragon, a mermaid, a dinosaur or a unicorn) and useful Italian words like some food, types of transport, animals, toys and clothes.

The 30 delightful pages all have borders and are single sided. On each page there are 3 or 4 Italian words, making a total of 100 Italian words throughout the whole book. Once completed, this will make a lovely book to refer back to. Ideal for ages 7 - 11.

ISBN 9781914159084

Also available by Joanne Leyland:

French
Young Cool Kids Learn French
First Words In French Teacher's Resource Book
Cool Kids Speak French (books 1, 2 & 3)
French Word Games - Cool Kids Speak French
40 French Word Searches Cool Kids Speak French
Photocopiable Games For Teaching French
First 100 Words In French Coloring Book Cool Kids Speak French
French at Christmas time
On Holiday In France Cool Kids Speak French
Cool Kids Do Maths In French
Un Alien Sur La Terre
Le Singe Qui Change De Couleur
Tu As Un Animal?

Italian
Young Cool Kids Learn Italian
Cool Kids Speak Italian (books 1, 2 & 3)
Italian Word Games - Cool Kids Speak Italian
40 Italian Word Searches Cool Kids Speak Italian
First 100 Words In Italian Coloring Book Cool Kids Speak Italian
On Holiday In Italy Cool Kids Speak Italian
Un Alieno Sulla Terra
La Scimmia Che Cambia Colore
Hai Un Animale Domestico?

German
Young Cool Kids Learn German
Cool Kids Speak German (books 1, 2 & 3)
German Word Games - Cool Kids Speak German
40 German Word Searches Cool Kids Speak German
First 100 Words In German Coloring Book Cool Kids Speak German

Spanish
Young Cool Kids Learn Spanish
First Words In Spanish Teacher's Resource Book
Cool Kids Speak Spanish (books 1, 2 & 3)
Spanish Word Games - Cool Kids Speak Spanish
40 Spanish Word Searches Cool Kids Speak Spanish
Photocopiable Games For Teaching Spanish
First 100 Words In Spanish Coloring Book Cool Kids Speak Spanish
Spanish at Christmas time
On Holiday In Spain Cool Kids Speak Spanish
Cool Kids Do Maths In Spanish
Un Extraterrestre En La Tierra
El Mono Que Cambia De Color
Seis Mascotas Maravillosas

English as a foreign language
Cool Kids Speak English (books 1 & 2)
First Words In English - 100 Words To Colour & Learn

The word search editions have 40 topics in each book. The word searches are in fun shapes. Pictures accompany the words to find.

The first 100 words colouring book editions have 3 or 4 words per page, and are ideal for those who like to colour as they learn.

The stories in a foreign language have an English translation at the back.

If you like games, you could try the word game editions.

The holiday editions have essential words & phrases in part 1. And in part 2 there are challenges to use these words whilst away.

For more information on the books available, and different ways of learning a foreign language go to https://learnforeignwords.com

Printed in Great Britain
by Amazon

83876786R00032